A GUIDE TO UNDRESSING YOUR MONSTERS

A GUIDE TO UNDRESSING YOUR MONSTERS

Sam Sax

Button Poetry / Exploding Pinecone Press
Minneapolis, Minnesota
2014

Published by Button Poetry / Exploding Pinecone Press,
Minneapolis, MN 55408

http://buttonpoetry.com

Manufactured in the United States of America

Internal Art: Akiva Levi

ISBN 978-0-9896415-4-8

TABLE OF CONTENTS

It is pointed out, regularly and endlessly, that the word "monster" shares roots with "monstrum," "monstrare," "monere"—"that which teaches," "to show," "to warn." This is true but no longer of any help at all, if it ever was.

—China Miéville

Are there many little boys who think they are a Monster? But in my case I am right.

—Anne Carson

פֿאַר וויבער און פֿאַר מאַנסבילן וואָס זיינען אַזוי ווי וויבער, דאָס הייסט זיי קענען ניט לערנען

BESTIARY

medusa—

when i saw my face / reduced & reddened / in his eyes
i turned / to stone / or a pillar of salt watching my village burn
he was the village / burning / maybe that's a different story
maybe in the end / only the snakes wept

mermaid—

half fish / half faggot / wishing for legs or the ocean / to open
like a mouth & swallow / all the fallen soldiers & seamen
i saved / a man / from his ship / fire in the water / brought him
to land / when i got my legs / he split me open anyway
said i was salt & slick / said my stink stank fresh

werewolf—

there are many words for transformation / metamorphosis
metaphor / medication / go to sleep / beside the man you love
& wake up next to a dog / maybe the moon brought it out of him
hound hungry for blood / maybe it's your fault / or maybe
it was there inside him / howling all along

RIBS

at the rib joint
we became men.

his whole body
smoked for ten hours

came apart
in my hands.

sucked the meat
off him. sucked
the bone. marrow
becomes you,
you know?

you know, when you eat
something, it becomes you?

younger me grew broccoli crowns from our skull,
grew hand antlers, ground ankle beef.

at the table
god unhinged his ribs
at the joint. opened him
like an oven laughing
with smoke, steam
flapping its black wings
up from his organs.

when i ate his ribs
i became a man

or maybe just ribs
braided together
at the table

or maybe a creation myth,

when i ate him.

in the beginning there was a table
i sat & ate at until i was something.

my reflection swallowed in the plate,
my god, the weight of the blade.

the blade, singing.

you know when you become
something it eats you? the teeth
in my hand. the weight of the handle.
the meat separating from bone.

CRUISING: A BROKEN TIARA

+

the night's thick with circling predators. i used to untie
myself and walk into its hunger. peel away fingers
until eyes climbed into back pockets, tongues
watered the sidewalk. in my wake, a field of belts

sprouted from the concrete, flailing their leathered
famine, patient to bind and to lash. the nights i walked
that desperate stretch until the sun unbuckled itself
from the dark—in the half-light i met many men

each with the same hands. i wore the night's bridle in
my hair, turning its axis, the backseats of taxi cabs
spilling over with limbs, flood of spit from between
the sewer's teeth, lips bit until they brayed and bled.

my god, my good god, to be a lamb again, dressed
in my finest garments, young, unsheered, pressed.

++

my god, my good god, to be a lamb again, dressed
for slaughter. before claws ripped through the beds
of my nails, before incisors split gums wide, before
eyes narrowed into the slits of a sickle, i was perfect.

my body, my good body, still wet with my mother's
last blood, legs red unfolding petals, graceless under
my torso. my whole hand wrapped around an index.
language a simple dance i'd learned to step inside.

but nostalgia always wears an ugly crown of teeth.
the greasy stain of my young body pressed between
encyclopedias, mouth a rash with no remedy, skin

the hungry codex i crawled out from within.

this street of one eyed gods, i'm the flashlight king.
this name moaned in the dark, the shadows sing.

+++

moan my name, the dark shadows sang back.
pressed against a brick wall in my thick coat
howling only when the boy's mouth was perfect,
a circle. i've been a man with many names.

he calls out the one scrawled inside my jacket,
that gleaming pocket watch, gold leaf over plastic,
hand over mouth, i bite down until blood flows
from his wrist, a signature claiming my lips.

when police shine their search light, it is perfect,
a circle. my throat a scarlet wound marked by the kill.
that boy, gone, clutching at the lamb folded in him.
me, a snarled wool stain awaiting interrogation.

i used to untie the night, before it swallowed me.
my god, my awful body, my good teeth.

HOW TO SPELL REDUCTIVE

what kind of man wears his limbs
like that? lunatic clock spinning
uneven arms until it's dark out.
how is it the same man always?

the one who does his simple violence
in an ohio janitor's closet, the one
who holds my wheezing body until
its breathing evens out. tell me

which man that is? the edge and the dull
back of a blade are both called *knife.*
who wears his body like a suit of arms?
tell me about testosterone's white lab

coat, how it barks through the cage's metal
bars. tell me a bruise can't mean
i love you, and i'll show you my neck
when he comes home from war.

i've never known a man who isn't both fist
and furniture. who wouldn't flip the switch
or perish in the kill shelter's poison.
i believe there is nothing

innate in the body. why every time a scientist
opens a child he finds only what he expected
to find. why when i splintered a bird's skull
with a brick in my young hands, a galleon

of bright wings spun out. why when my brother
saw that mess of red feathers gasping
in my palm, two expressions crossed
his face at the same time.

WHEN RESEARCHING PUBLIC SEX THEATRES FOR A POEM

you know you have to pay, right?
    the marquee does its neon work to draw you
        but your wallet will be punished.

the big man sits in his tiny booth with his big hands.
    you wonder if he finds you disgusting or sees you.
        place the bill right in his palm, feel meat

through the currency. fantasize he might follow you in,
    leave your eyes in his mouth. what is a poem worth, anyway?
        ten dollars at the door? the long stair case? the soiled

cloth seats? who uses cloth seats anymore, anyway?
    you read they hold disease better than mosquitoes,
        feel the swarm beneath as you sit,

each tiny needle sucking you down. it is dark
    as you imagined. but you do not do what you imagined
        you would do. your body does not transform

into something with more limbs, prehensile and guttural.
    you sit. hands decorative silk napkins folded in pockets.
        the whole of your skin shrinking away from its lineage.

that accordion history opening all its doors into the dark.
    imagine the actors dead now, forever blazing in celluloid
        before the swarms of us, forced into the same positions

over and over. the desperate cocaine buzzing through
    the screen, the same angry hives, the overdubbed screams.
        in the pause between films, you wonder again,

the cost of a poem. is it the man wearing a dark
    suit beside you? his face a candle of legs? his wet, demanding
        lips? the next film begins… and you reach out for him.

the mosquito's feeding blood forward into your hands.
    your hands, outstretched as though you'd expect him to save
        you. but he pulls away. he fades into the dark. then,

when you open your mouth one strange voice stumbles out
    after another. pandemic of hair yawns down your back, a thin
        tail gasps out from between your hind legs. so you walk

down the long staircase. your body transforming to something
    so much smaller. the big man's hands now five stories wide.
        in the cab ride home, you laugh at how you tried to speak

a dying language. how naive and brave you were.
    how ludicrous you believed you might find something holy
        in sweat, a new way to talk about perversion or release

or the genealogy of desire. you don't tell anyone you went. so tiny
    you could climb into a stranger's pocket. and you want to.
        and you paid to. ugly swarm of cloth still folded in the blood.

isn't it funny how you once believed nothing
in this whole world could disgust you?

BESTIARY

big foot—

my mother wants / to know what my man looks like
but he's camera shy / he's bipedal humanoid
he's illusive / which signifies / he's ashamed
it's a sham / that kind of man / when it gets serious
disappears

candy man—

who fears mirrors / my man & i / stare at our reflection
& make a cute couple / which means / with his arm around me
we look / like the kind of faggots / you wouldn't want to see
dead / but somewhere inside him / waiting / for the right words
to be said / is a butcher

siren—

he cries / & i / lashed to the mast of a ship / steer my body
toward the sound / sheets bound around wrists & ankles
tears make grief / a lighthouse you wear / when i hear him
a huge wood wheel turns in my stomach / & i break
open on his jagged coast

THE HUNGER ARTIST

the boy ate from my hands
then ate my hands,

finger bones making old
noises between his teeth,

my arm in his mouth down
to the elbow, the shoulder.

he gnaws through the sinew
strung up in my neck

like a white upright piano.
it sounds terrible

when he eats, all those
depressed keys

making music. each organ
forging sound. his windpipe

a well that drowns bright
boys like coins with dead

blues singers' faces stamped
in the metal. fathomless pit,

cannibal ditch, the father,
the son, & the holy spirit

spread across his fingers
& lips.

the job of any competent
parasite is to convince

its host of their relationship's

symbiosis. i loved him even

as the anesthetic went in,
hatchet lifted from a hymnal,

& when i was at last inside him,
i couldn't make a sound.

FISHING

we stole fish from the ocean,
butchered, threw them back in pieces
on hooks. the two of us: me and daniel with grease in his hair
on a dock that reached out
      into the water like a man with broken arms,
wood rotting in his arms. daniel
  with oiled hair,   with a throat like a lighthouse,
sometimes i think all he was
        was eyes. the kind that roll up into the skull
like a map   that will burn before they show you   water.

fish don't have throats to cut, so we stabbed
      wildly. my first knife, bright as a smile, sectioned their
seizing bodies. my smile, my knife.
          daniel and i.   worked with no care
   for their anatomy, for the proper way to make them
open. perhaps, our forearms touched
     as guts spilled through our fingers
as we slid hooks through their skins
      as we threw them back in
and pulled out fish that looked just like them
       as if the ocean had pieced them back together.

that night we slept
     in his mother's house. in the dark, i ran my fingers through
his hair, brought them to my face and tasted salt.

i wanted so badly
     to be a knife then. to take him
apart in pieces. to throw him back
        in the ocean.

or perhaps, i wanted to take him
     into my mouth, to feel something sharp
break inside of me,
      to be pulled up
        into the screaming air,
          somehow whole.

HEAVY PETTING

frottage: (frô-täzh') *n.* from the old french *frotter,* to rub

is the ugliest word in our english language, hands down, the way it feels in the mouth when you speak it.

the act itself is fine. two or more bodies rubbing their clothed or nude frames against each other like bloodied coats. fur, curves, fat, cursive, burrow, all sounds lovely. but frottage: cottage cheese, curdled milk, mottled bird, molted clot.

the verb is *to frot.* he and i frotted. we frotted so hard the couch lost a layer of skin. his mother came in and caught us frottaging.

i suppose in the throes one can say almost anything and the sweat will make it hot. but why words that don't sound how they mean? why words that make the body obscene? why not let the throat make new each act that happens to it? the vocal chords a chorus of naming and invention.

the phrase *dry humping* makes me want to gag when i speak it. i think it's the vowel sounds: the ump, the umping, the to ump. gag, on the other hand, is a great word. it sounds exactly how it happens. an action choked out of the body or down into it vibrating on desire's thin repulsive wire.

i first learned the word *frottage* getting tested for sti's after the last man did what he wanted with my silence. i didn't have words then, or the right ones. they told me nothing could be transmitted from what happened. that his trans-ness meant no violence could be left inside.

so what was i meant to do with all this sick?

17

how to carry or name it?

the other meaning of frottage is a technique of
obtaining an impression by placing a piece of paper
over an object, rubbing it with charcoal, until you steal
its shape. this is most common with gravestones and
funerary monuments.

that sounds about right.
that sounds exactly how it happened.

RECOGNIZING YOUR MONSTERS

on the days i was convinced it was my brother
and not me who was the monster, i imagined
all the ways i could destroy him. always began
with the image of him reaching out to kiss me
like something other than a brother and ended
with him dressed in blood, limbs threaded down
the street, my hands the color of a matador's cape.

little prince, cruel justice, sword polished
to a mirror's sheen. what do you do with a brother
born with the head of a bull? can the hero destroy
him without being destroyed? blood ties worn
around the neck, blood shines like a mirror
with a crack in it.

once, he asked me if i thought he was handsome,
we were driving home, my eyes scythed in the rearview
preparing for war, readied my hands to rope around
his neck, the car tumbling over the guardrail, imagined
it'd go right on floating up into the air like we were
some other pair of brothers. the car with burning
wings. neither of us would come out alive.

on the days i was convinced it was my brother
and not me who was the faggot, i dreamed all the ways
to make him die. to look in his bull eyes
and see someone else there.

BESTIARY

golem—

take his hair in your hands / his dead
skin cells / his discarded undergarments / take them
& make of them a new boy / this effigy / his likeness & nothing
like him / breathe life / into its clenched carapace / my god
i think i saw it / move

moloch—

latex / rolled over / the nursery / depository / for children
my bull headed man / anthropomorphized / every time / i come
inside him / is sacrifice

troll—

who hasn't loitered below bridges / surveyed the waiting dark
for a boy to pass / to make him / disappear / who hasn't made
a home in the groaning echo / under the overpass / dined
on spears / clenched the tense corridor of the spine
ran their tongue over fangs / tasted god

FOLKTALE

in the beginning god said let there be god and there was god.
in ukraine, the winters were so cold we told stories about fire:
the four swordsman on their burning horses, their burning swords.
king solomon and his flaming underpants, and my personal favorite,
the old men who gave birth to baked bread. my zedee told me this
story from her creaking wood body buried in her creaking
wood chair. goes like this:

there weren't always radiators, sam. all these shower heads
you crank open like a dragon's wet mouth. you don't know
cold, sam. san francisco has but one season, it's called *easy.*
even in new york, we watch winter stampede toward us from
our hi-tec down coats, electric blankets wrapped around our
skulls for head scarves. in the old country we'd have to rub
our legs together how crickets sing to find love and this is
how we kept warm. also, this is how we made love. we kept
warm all the time. this is how your father was born. some
days you'd look out into the cabbage and see people laid out
in great big heated pyramids, rubbing their legs against each
other, some possessed orchestra, a maggid's accordion, a field
of rocking chairs.

of course a lot of babies came during that next snow year. so
many mouths frozen shut. of course there was much sadness,
tears hardening on the face. so the town decided to pass a law
stating that when we laid together for warmth, men and
women slept separate.

i don't know if you know this sam but when two men make
love, they also make bread. the slow yeast and butter, yolks
breaking in the hand, sugar poured until it makes you sick,
you understand this, i know you do, i've read your poems. and
you know the older the man the richer the bread. so hashem
rose the body temperature of these men until they all sang
like ovens. they labored indoors and birthed perfect loaves.
that winter, we ate how kings eat. we feasted on the meat of
onions, sliced at the dark bread that tasted like my father's

24

heaven. that bread leavened before our homes were leveled by men on burning horses, who took our boys away to feed the furnace of empire.

the moral of this story is that for someone who has no bread, no house, and no love, rubbing against a rich old man aint that bad. i know you know this sam, i've read your poems.

but also, that there are many ways to value labor, to eat and be eaten by love. there are miracles inside us, you see this in how we are here, sam. how we survived the cold unbroken and became something else entirely, not flame, not match head with countless wood bodies, not fire escape drooling gasoline, but something that rises in the heat.

MASTURBATING IN THE SYNAGOGUE BATHROOM

the difference between men and women i'm told early on somehow happens in bathrooms. in my synagogue there was a single bullet hole in the mirror above the men's room sink or at the time i imagined it the perfect splintered circle of an absent god's mouth pursed and kissing his own reflection. this is how i've learned to understand men.

the women's bathroom was a more elaborate place. i remember crimson ornamentation dripping from the ceiling, ottoman with her fat plush beard, cloth napkins folded by three pristine mirrors. this is how i remember it. why i am always trying to crawl back inside. why i was scolded with smiling arms by the rabbi for mistaking that room for mine.

oh sam—you are such a good boy.

and here i am in this ugly stall again
pulling myself apart. wrenching my skin
up to heaven, a collection of nerve endings
breaking down. i can hear my family cry out
for forgiveness in a huge room to a dead book,
my right hand, a bullet wound, the mouth
of an absent god. my god my cock is a hideous thing
pressed between all these holy books. my god
is a man with a dozen bleeding mouths. a prayer,
an explosion of cold letters. a new white flower
for my black suit jacket

OLD WIVES' TALE

the man bathed in milk and became beautiful,
then a mule, then a man again, then left.

he spread red paint over his lips and went out
dancing. knew i always hated

how we varnish our mouths in blood. *light a candle.*
remember we had no measuring cups

in ukraine. sectioned out flour by the fistful,
made for lumpy bread but bread all the same.

all the old magic we used to be pretty. slaughtered
goat and cindered village, something

worth something better rise from them ashes. boy,
a glowing candle on that dark floor,

gone out. wore other men's hair in his hair. *say*
your lover's dead name five times

into a mirror. if only the old curses still worked,
i could have swapped his reliquary

for a dibbuk box, poured salt around his sneakers,
sliced his cheek to boil in milk 'til he muled.

TEETH

how elegant, the disarticulated human skull
where steel makes one fused bone many.

the mandible is a planter's box outside my cold room in ohio:
the converted nursing home where old folks from poland
and romania are all now trapped in the lights
or trapped in the white paint.

+

antique sciences of the mouth
can teach the history of science
more than anything about the mouth.
for centuries lancets and leaches
were used on infant gums
to assist teething, animal bone rattles
drowned in mercury powder,
a white gloved hand doing damage
in a child's bright mouth.

+

my teeth are mine. felt them rise up under my tongue.
wisdom came last. replaced each tiny forbearer.

forgot they grew where their parents died. so i am not
surprised they ache and rot now, they scream when flooded
with something sweet they do not deserve.

this is what happens when you forget your history,
the journey that brought you to the mouth, the labor
in the enamel, the tongue with no name,

when all you are is white.

BESTIARY

ghost—

is not a monster / but neither is the conqueror
from the conqueror's mouth / nostalgia is a mausoleum
full of men / whose images i've loved / more than their skeletons
what is a ghost but what thrives / outside the body
what is the heart / but a haunting / but a looted museum

vampire—

hepatitis / west nile / malaria / hiv / what can't be carried
like a burning torch / through the blood / what gift
ribbons the skin / turns the chest / endowment
hunger punctures this cistern of a neck / what else
do you forget / to save / each time / you're fed

zombie—

what puppets / empty meat to the club & compels it / to dance
what crystal / what ice / what glass / what speed / what laughter
sounds like slowed down / & deadened / flesh / his body / moves
as if possessed / by spirits / he's invincible / now / he's already
gone

HANDS

there is a pit bull chained in the basement.
there is a big-bang chained to my limp wrist.
there is a banging in the pipes in the basement
and the dog is chained down there.

four dogs have passed through this world
through my hands. my hands are bad at keeping
things alive. they're bad dogs, my hands shit
in the house and sneak out to fuck in the street.

my father once tied his brother to a radiator
mid-winter and left him all night. charles' skin
was singed down through to the bone,
my hands have bad blood in them.

they held a spoon over a lighter's white blade
and made a mess of my upper leg. i watched
my bark swallow the scar in its maw. my hands
love to make war of love. they make off

with all the gold rings and make brass knuckles
blunt. how my fist sliced at that wiry kid until
he was trained to lower his eyes. how they locust
at any boy who's just started to bear limes.

there is a pit bull chained in my hands, he screams
like a tooth dressed in gold. he is a boy or a dog
or an animal with louder grief. my hands cannot unchain
that beast or hold his matted coat until his heart stops

sprinting. my hands know only one kind of labor. two
fingers slipped in past the knuckle, three if i've been fed
liquor. they are selfish gods. they know every word
for pleasure but only one for give. my gasp and my galaxy.

a new myth in which my hands are put down
at the wrist. where the bone is cut off at the elbow
and thrown to the hounds. a new constellation
where a boy drags his dead dog across the night sky.

IT'S ALIVE!

try & watch a horror film
from the point of view
of the monster.   imagine,
every man shrieks at the sight
of you, children throw stones
& laugh at your blood, a mob
forms   on your   doorstep
with pitchforks & forceps
just for fun or from fear.
this is your wretched life.
you didn't know your name
until they named you. didn't
know your teeth were fangs
until they tried to pry them
from your pliant skull, didn't
know your hunger was so
unclean. so you learned to
grow in the dark as darkness
grew in you. your mirror
a massacre of light, your
appearance   a   film   reel
perverted in flames. it's not
til you love a boy & make him
like you   that you're able
to curse   the civilization
that assembled your fiction,
to gaze upon your own
grotesque elegance & laugh,
to love the rough-hewn battle
of your haggard breath. you
child of the axe blade
buried in your breast, you
story men tell to explain away
the darkness & give it depth.
you apotheosis of the oldest
protest   hymn.   what is
the ocean besides a puddle

without you in it? what is
the grim forest   besides
a factory of trees praying to be
sheared into paper? what is
your mouth but a home, but
a haunted motel, but a siren
of terrible righteous noise.
now the men who once
tormented you,   tremble
at your sound, dark horse
mounting its unkind rider
& when you're finally ready
to spread wide your wild red
wings, it ends. some idiot girl
pierces your faggot carapace
with her car,   or sword,
or word in a dead language
for fun, from fear & audiences
in darkened theatres release
a   collective   sigh of relief
as you perish, as credits roll
back like eyes & you're
reminded this is a movie,
you die onscreen every night.
try & get to that last scene
without laughing or weeping
or eating the dark alive.

PRESCRIPTION POPPIES

16.

perfect, to escape in whiteness.
        under the counter cabinet medicines.
                the body, dreaming only of itself.

what numbness carries its burning
        spotlight through my starless blood?
                what science can bottle a stoned

eucharist? let me lay here another hundred
        years, until each knuckle grows a tiny beard.
                both eyes burrowing into the dark

television, comforted by its darkness.
        let me lay here, mother standing above me,
                her face slack as an umbilical cord.

she holds a million tiny white eggs
        inside her, each one a bottled god.
                an orange bottle empty in her palm.

god mother, you're blocking the screen.
        calm mother, i'm dulled by the pharmacy.
                i swallowed ten perfect white eggs.

each one hatched suns in my stomach.
        the children of distilled smoke dragons,
                can't you see them? their ten warm yolks

singing heat to my blood. your first
        grandsons numb as my young body
                slung across the floor.

aren't you amazed at how quiet i lay?
        at how much labor goes into the terminus.
                congratulations!

it's a boy.

26.

careful sam, remember this body
       is your last. already, so many friends
              have damaged their wiring or flooded

entirely. twenty six is the year before talented
       people die. thank goodness you've had
              to work at this. sweating over the page

until it became something. equilibrium
       is no high. good, you've stopped profiteering
              off your friend's injuries.

every mouth surgery and broken rib was
       a beacon glittering and pornographic
              in the distance. your salt muscle pulling

toward sustenance. when your lover
       gifts you a wreath of medicines for your birthday,
              with his brother's sick name etched

into the bottle. *stop.* even when your tongue
       sweats a famished gutter, know tongues
              are supposed to water. what alchemy turns

gold leaf to bare trees. it is a war,
       you know, the body pitted against itself.
              the brain refusing to flood

this desiccated blood, unless you pray
       to the appropriate gods. i've knelt for years
              at a time before strange medicine cabinets,

swallowed entire beehives for a single
       drop of honey. after all the opium
              has been burned from the water,

after the smoke clears over this flaming
       apiary of a home, know you will only be left
              with what you were born with

your breath.
your clean blood.
your green bones.

MONSTER COUNTRY

god bless all policemen & their splintering night sticks splintering & lord have mercy on their souls. god bless judges in their empty robes who send young men off to prisons with a stain from their antiquated pens. god bless all the king's monsters & all the kings men. god bless the sentence & its inevitable conclusion. god bless the predators, curators of small sufferings. god bless the carpet that ate one hundred dollars of chris's cocaine. god bless cocaine & the colophon of severed hands it takes to get to your nostrils. god bless petroleum & coffee beans & sugar cane & rare earth minerals used to manufacture music boxes. god bless the gas chamber & the gas that makes the shower head sing. god bless the closet i trapped a terrified girl in with my two good hands. god bless the night those good boys held my face to a brick wall & god bless those boys & good god bless the strange heat that pressed back.

> you cannot beg
> for forgiveness
> with a mouth

BESTIARY

charybdis—

when i suck in / i make deadly / whirlpools / ask anyone
who's managed / to climb out / alive

cyclops—

it happens / at least once / to everyone / focused
on another person's pleasure / leave the body / in the path
of oncoming traffic / tithe with two good eyes / at a man's wet
altar / spirits rise up / like a school of dead / fish inside him
in the land of the blind / the one-eyed man is queen

dragon—

patrol or pillage / he exhales & a whole village
burns / iron-scaled sentry / guardian of the ivory
tower i wrap my legs around / everyone
thinks / he's just a brute / but for me
he lifts his breast plate / for me
he welcomes the quiver / & the arrow's teeth

BUTTHOLE

oh putrid rose. oh floral gift from some dead god
i buried alive only to excavate and find, still fresh.

oh myriad sweet sounds i make with it: trumpet,
trombone, tornado, goblin. oh mouth

that gapes and swallows. oh mouth that hungers
for new tongue. oh stomach that rests so far from

the colon but still calls him cousin. oh come, oh old
world magic, oh small hungry prince.

how many octaves can you tuba? how many eloquent
speeches come right from the gut? what countless

phallic shapes have you named husband? what knuckle
tucked into you a dyke holding up all this stale water.

sweet you, who birthed iron when i took too many
women's multivitamins claiming there's no such thing

as gender. praise, how you expand and shrink like
a house's water pipes from winter into its heat. praise

how when you bleed you're always trying to tell me
something. praise you, tiny gymnast, beast

with a breathing halo, gold band that weds my strange
body to this strange strange earth

PUTTING ON EMILY DICKINSON'S CLOTHES

i take her discarded bone ribbed corset
& let it give me all the curves of a hand
written poem. pin my black hair up
into an arrogant shape. take a pair of hard
wood shoes & force each foot inside.
i blush & rouge, write sparse rhymed
lines, powder my face white, tie a black
tippet around my throat, fit three fingers
inside deep as they go, each one mine.
i turn up the church hymns & dance
without moving my hips. my empty room,
my audience. yes, the body of the poet, thin
pale eucharist, transubstantiation of flesh
into flesh. even the replica white frilled
garment hanging on a mannequin in her
home is only a replica. i step in & raise
its roof beams, it fits like a reverie worth
reveling inside or just a dead woman's dress.
i take & take until there is only a white
woman folded in her sunday best in a white
cabinet locked in the dark ground. you can't
wear your mother's clothes without becoming
your mother. you can't take on her voice
without also taking her hands & throat.
even boarded up in the body i am still
staring out of windows.

HEART

grandpa's exploded right inside him
    can of gray paint in the carburetor

flames   up through the hood

he collapsed on some woman's steps
    a shock of flower's wilting in his fist
i love this story so much
  i placed the flowers in his hand myself
                    made them red

better love's last dying declaration
than an apology   that never got spoken
or a broken man   begging
a place to sleep   the night

i try not to think of my own heart

its constant unflinching labor
                  its loft inside my throat

its four chambers
that will one day unbraid
             into my coffin

whenever a lover beats out
              its thin cortège
on my breast   his ear pressed against me
listening for a stampede
        of long extinct mammoth
i'm sure it will stop   while he listens

i'm sure my breath   will leave me
as he pounds at the dead flower
in my chest.
       how tragic that he will go
on living

BOYS & BRIDGES

we were new at playing gods, it was easy to tell.
    the world broken in two categories: flame & melt.
        we may have actually believed it, we may still.

when i get down on me knees i become
    a boy again, snap my fingers & elevators open
        their old legs, hold my hand above a highway

deem the river continue to flow. back then,
    my friends would grip my neck & kill me
        then help me rise from death. switch blade

in an electric socket, river of pills & paint,
    painted rivers spilling from nostrils, open
        veins, police stations of the cross

hallucinations pulled from a church's back lot.
    tell me what kind of boys don't want to master
        fire? who can blame the blaze on anything

but our sweat. forget everything swallowed by it.
    mother pocketing my book of matches,
        forgetting my birth name for detectives.

in one field there's a dog buried below the corn.
    it was there because of us, still is. once it opened
        its mouth to howl & all of god's green dirt

spilled in. below another field are thousands
    of families. they are also there because of us, for less
        obvious reasons. picking the food from our teeth

to eat how any god eats, without a care for what dirt
    grows the meat. we learned all this from the river,
        indoor kids on a white water raft wearing bright

orange life jackets. below a bridge, the man
    who was meant to guide us through the wilderness
        pulled up a bag from below the black water

untied its burlap mouth & a dog's wet body
    spilled out. of course we blamed the man for this,
        of course we tried to become him, of course we burned

that wood to the ground. went home to our undrowned
    dogs. felt their wet blood on fire inside them. lost in
        our town, a new forest. we're still climbing out.

NOTES

"The Hunger Artist" is from a series written after Franz Kafka's short story.

"Recognizing your Monsters" is written after Laura Lamb Brown-Lavoie.

"Folktale" is written after Marge Piercy

"Prescription Poppies" is following Sylvia Plath

The first line of "Monster Country" *god bless all policemen* comes from "Goodbat Nightman" by Roger McGough.

"Putting on Emily Dickinson's Clothes" is in response to "Taking off Emily Dickinson's Clothes" by Billy Collins

SPECIAL THANKS TO

Hieu Minh Nguyen, Cam Awkward-Rich, Brigit Pegeen Kelly, Naomi Shihab Nye, Michael McGriff, Carrie Fountain, Dean Young, all the folks at The Michener Center for Writers, Sean Patrick Mulroy, Katelyn Lucas, Tim 'Toaster' Henderson, Akiva Levi, Nic Alea, Danez Smith, Fatimah Asghar, Franny Choi, Eduardo Corral, Spitshine, Calslam, Chen Chen, The Bay Area Poetry Community, The great folks at Button Poetry particularly Michael Mlekoday, Sam Cook, most of all to my family, Matthew Sax, Hollis Rafkin-Sax, & Ben Sax. Love you all,

without y'all this book would not be possible.

ACKNOWLEDGMENTS

Acknowledgment is made to the journals in which these poems first appeared, sometimes under different titles:

Anti-: "Boys & Bridges" and "Old Wives' Tale"

Berkeley Poetry Review: "Folktale"

Devil's Lake: "How to Spell Reductive"

Drunk in a Midnight Choir: "Bestiary" (selections), "It's Alive!," and "Teeth"

Four Way Review: "Monster Country"

Gertrude: "Ribs"

The Journal: "Fishing"

Muzzle Magazine: "Cruising: A Broken Tiara," "Masturbating in the Synagogue Bathroom," and "Butthole"

PANK: "Prescription Poppies"

Rattle: "When Researching Public Sex Theaters for a Poem"

Smoking Glue Gun: "Hands" and "The Hunger Artist"

Tandem: "Heavy Petting"

Weave: "A Guide to Recognizing Your Monsters"

Word Riot: "Heart" and "Putting on Emily Dickinson's Clothes"

ABOUT THE AUTHOR

sam sax is a fellow at The Michener Center for Writers, the two-time Bay Area Unified Grand Slam Champion, and the two-time Oakland Grand Slam Champion. He is a recipient of The Acker Award in Poetry and co-founded the reading series The New Sh!t Show, which is currently running in four cities across the United States. His poems have appeared or are forthcoming in *Rattle*, *The Journal*, *The Minnesota Review*, *Vinyl*, and other journals, and he is unspeakably thrilled that you are holding his book in your hands.